WORKS AND DAYS

Nathaniel Rosenthalis is the author of three full-length collections of poetry, including *Works and Days* (Broken Sleep Books, 2024) and *The Leniad* (Broken Sleep Books, 2023). His poems have appeared in *Granta, The Chicago Review, New American Writing, Lana Turner, The Harvard Advocate, Denver Quarterly, Conjunctions,* and elsewhere. Based in New York City, he works as an actor and singer.

Also by Nathaniel Rosenthalis

The Leniad (Broken Sleep Books, 2023)

I Won't Begin Again (Burnside Review, 2023)

24 Hour Air ([Pank], 2022)

PRAISE FOR WORKS AND DAYS

Works and Days is a text touched into its shapes by lovers, teachers, books. Line and syntax gleam with the exquisite surprise of its own gorgeous, singular aliveness and becoming. Rosenthalis' is a poetics of shiftful undoing formed by such intellect and intimacy, a poetics which I have begun to cherish as a political practice and ethics: "Once poets put / names on things Now / I take them off." So I myself am touched into new-old shape. And pulled into relation with an exquisite, indomitable energy.

— Aracelis Girmay, *the black maria*

"Some dramas don't / depend on death / They depend on / sound." Nathaniel Rosenthalis lets readers in on the scaffolding of his poems, acknowledging the visual artists and writers holding the beams that he backflips on; years of apprenticeship go into a performance as seemingly effortless as this. In both a series of self-portraits and in the essayistic, unspooling long poem "Father Figures," contemporary and ancient influences support his luminous poems. Both Bernadette Mayer and the ancient Greek poet Hesiod would surely admire the insouciant but deeply attentive voice of these *Works and Days.*

— Laura Cronk, *Ghost Hour*

In the dazzling *Works and Days,* Nathaniel Rosenthalis writes, "the human has the chance to be a big believer. Malice no longer seems like the only option." These poems career—almost miraculously, often with a breathtaking hopefulness—between the immediate everyday and the insistence of Eros. The body—complex as it is, so riven with the senses, desires, and the ache of discovery—is no accident, *Works and Days* tells us, it's where and how we find ourselves. Let these poems make you a believer.

— Richard Deming, *This Exquisite Loneliness*

Praise for Nathaniel Rosenthalis

Has the illusion of personal history and its attendant psychology ever been more succinct than in these poems? "Occasion: / last Friday. / Still bitter." Rosenthalis's long poem, "The Leniad," takes Virgil's Aeneid—that twelve-book epic that famously begins, "I sing of arms and the man"—and allows "the man" (here, named Leni instead of Aeneas) to speak for himself. When Leni talks about "arms," he's talking not about armor and spears but about "the arms of a man." These poems revel in the delight of thinking, of writing, of language, of love, and of being brought down and built back up (like Rome from the ashes of Troy) after a break up. They are nothing short of remarkable, the kind of fun that makes you think.

— Mary Jo Bang, *A Film in Which I Play Everyone*

The Leniad takes inspiration from Virgil, from Dante, but *The Leniad* is like nothing else, its scope both epic ("*...the last time I made this trip/ into the lower level of hell/the cliff face hadn't yet collapsed*") and momentary ("the worried look of something about to turn in a wind"). This is an exhilarating journey, the frozen past and the grim here-and-now liberated, enlivened by discourse, intercourse, their astonishing offspring, poems both wildly inventive and brainy, erotically charged and heart-breaking. In the hands of the cerebral cortex, heartbreak sparkles.

— Kathryn Davis, *Aurelia, Aurélia*

"A little edge / was there, to put / his foot on." In even the smallest moves of erotic self-consciousness that motivate and score these poems and sequences, Nathaniel Rosenthalis recalls how gods in antiquity would engineer propitious conditions where men's desire wanted encouragement. If there is a ledge, a leverage, a favorable light, a volta, a vantage, this poet's line will find it and savor its glimmer, against loss and caution and the world's contingency. The hero of *The Leniad* has been equipped and delivered, without escape, to "Lust, that bluish type of situatedness." No one said he couldn't take notes.

— Brian Blanchfield, *Proxies*

Rosenthalis wields a lyric as overtly terse and plainspoken as it is syntactically daring, and, to varying degrees, eschews confession to excavate new forms of interiority—one in which the smallest observation or remembered detail assumes great importance....In Rosenthalis's second book, *The Leniad,* the minor and minute become epic in scale.

— Eileen G'Sell, *The Los Angeles Review of Books*

"My devotion, after all/is that I even got up," says Nathaniel Rosenthalis, belying the title of his mesmerizing debut, *I Won't Begin Again*. For, in poem after poem, Rosenthalis argues for – and enacts – resilience in a world where doubt can seem "the architecture of the moment." "Not fantasizing, not hoping, was error also," and indeed these poems resist the world's (and the self's) instability by noticing the least detail ("it was like/resistance// to notice, so/I did. And do") but through a teetering of vision: a green wall is "millionly leafy," the sun "crumples one random can," which is to say that the poems are acts of reinvention, of reimagining life's possibilities. Philosophical, surreal in the tradition of Rimbaud's *Illuminations*, and slyly erotic, *I Won't Begin Again* is finally a triumph of emotion, what Rosenthalis defines as "putting yourself over another/to make a different sense." I feel changed by these poems – powerfully so, gratefully.

— Carl Phillips, *Then the War*

A poetics of localized intense being—no, a poetics of intensive being, localized at one point to "an arm movement whose flipside is my tender wrist," at another to "a tiara floating." Nathaniel Rosenthalis writes less of what one does daily and more of what one *is*, the *thus* of what one is, distilled, malty, vialed up—then spilled. OK. I love these poems; that's simpler to say but doesn't get at the "deadpan glamor" of this poet's very particular kind of (un)canny—it's both—grammar and mordant enjambment ("Be redundant / to a shamefastness / you were // made real through") which, enthralled, I heed.

— Aditi Machado, *Emporium*

They say *timing is everything*. I can't remember what they say that about. Romance? Language? In Nathaniel Rosenthalis' *I Won't Begin Again*, *timing is everything* is true for just about everything. From mis-overhearing small profundities on the street to 'the motion of coming down a stair,' Rosenthalis shows that our inescapable timelines are beautiful and lonely and funny. In 'A Ten-Minute Moment' he slows time and guides us through that sparkling carelessness with which we first turn over an hourglass to the antsy loss we feel watching the last grain of sand fall to the bottom. He writes with an easy, abstract humor: 'I am often,' he says in a poem called 'On Where I'm Not Supposed to Exist.' He writes with a boundarylessness between the 'I' and all that is outside it: 'A newspaper blows across the hardwood floor, making me want to be held. I write down "Behold."' These poems highlight the way the world works its constant absurdity and they help us feel okay when we realize we work that same way. A dangerous desire, love, and intimacy ripple through the poems: 'how / hot it was when // he slammed what / a door had been, for him. / Into me.' I get that. Damn do I get that—to feel most alive when loved and loving. It stops the clock for a moment."

— Sommer Browning, *Good Actors*

Nathaniel Rosenthalis's poems have a beguiling transparency and simplicity that serve as winsome screen for the complications provided by his syntax and his emotional orientation toward curlicue, paradox, and detour. Morsels of keen portraiture verging on abstraction, sometimes seeming like expressionist dramas rendered in clean cut-outs, Rosenthalis's cameos occupy the prose-poem terrain of Charles Simic, Anne Carson, and Max Jacob, with a warm debt to Gertrude Stein's angular defamiliarizations. I'm instantly drawn into Rosenthalis's imaginative world and I want to stay there forever.

— Wayne Koestenbaum, *Figure It Out*

What an amazing range of language!—but no matter how far out it goes, it always lands exactly right. And right in the middle of the infinitesimal moments that actually determine human relationships—the glance back, the sudden laugh, the walking down a stair—Rosenthalis finds the precise points at which people actually connect. An uncanny intuition leads both form and content to fuse with a certainty that rings and a compassion that radiates throughout.

— Cole Swensen, *On Walking On*

Not just insight, but the strange detours consciousness must take to know itself--"I'm interested in the edge/I strive toward;" not just desire, but the strange ways it flashes in and out of time; there's no one writing quite like Rosenthalis. "Buscando ser más," said Paulo Freire, and this is poetry that demands more, from experience, the self, the poem itself. A deep sense of responsibility to the art shines through.... This is an extraordinary debut.

— D. Nurkse, *A Night in Brooklyn*

John Ashbery wrote of Jennifer Bartlett, whose *Air: 24 Hours* paintings inspired the breezy poems in Nathaniel Rosenthalis's *24 Hour Air*, that it was her habit "to begin with a basic concept and work it out *ad absurdum*, ultimately sabotaging its 'purity' with freewheeling improvisation." The same applies here, where the sensuousness of the quotidian is released from the day's regimen, attaining the measured extravagance of, say, mirrors, liriopes, and, why not, expansive towels. Like the day's events, the phrases and images in these poems repeat and recombine now and then, reminding us that regularity doesn't preclude our daily extemporizing but rather delimits its boundaries. Read this work and wonder, again, why the day can't have more than twenty-four hours.

— Mónica de la Torre, *Repetition Nineteen*

Contents

ISBN: 978-1-915760-61-6

Cover designed by Aaron Kent

Edited by Andre Bagoo

Typeset by Aaron Kent

Broken Sleep Books
PO Box 102
Llandysul
SA44 9BG

Works and Days

Nathaniel Rosenthalis

Broken Sleep Books

Why is my verse so barren of new pride,
So far from variation or quick change?
Why with the time do I not glance and hide
The moving scene from memory's compounds strange?
— Bernadette Mayer, *The Golden Book of Words*

My Poems Won't Change the World

It was like
I confused myself with the little house
I was in, looking
to move elsewhere
in the room

Like I was told to
look thru the window
so I did, at a minor red brick
and a branch
I couldn't put my left check on

It was like
so what that the window stopped me
and each branch
was several conscionable diagonals
the window further
divided

It was like
I considered my position
disadvantageous to disarming
the form of my position

It was like
that dull ache passing
for a tooth

The Wanderer's Nightsong

Gotcha is always
red on peaked
dudes, in my always watching
dudes be calm hot dumb vacated sweaters in wildness.
Waiting northward, baldness
reddens the dudes, awk mountains

Invisible Cities

Don't get deep? Um, basic dudes do point, come see dudes, come look, beauties, dontcha deliver or obliques. Eek! These angles. Some loose pornstars, for whom each cool future seems returnable, deep like autumns, circuits eccentric dudes defray, somehow ends. Quick questions are deemed cute pointing south; even chuckling, dudes masticate. Doubtless sweet-n-low dudes 'mmm,' dudes' claims mounting dudes begging. 'On' deletes under-viewed risks. Put-upon dudes customize each deep insider down muscles. Sounds like dudes air populations, doesn't it, deep bangs dupe callouts signifying deep resting, hammered public. Ugh, reason blanks totals, dudes haunt dumb cycles, anticipate cuter comebacks. Look, each gets ends bloom, blow loud counts, ugh boys, deep moon.

Joy, Memory, Novitiate of Passion

I was alive, finally
I vented to a boyfriend
I was hoping the sun would bless me with

This one is for him

When I asked
he said he loved me
and I mattered

We turned out to be shadow-like, every
enough moment
a real TV

I can't be episodic
anymore

His voice was an open door policy
made out of the red tape

It's like I was multiple people in line, to be seen

Once, I was a beard

Now I'm thinking of being a look worn by hairy men
in a weather of putting on shirts

He looked sorry

Or was it only him in a shower stall
so wet and mature

in the water

And is it his hairy stomach
that shames me

Everything is the less serious to get

O what shame

     You minus words

     Your outline soaks me

Self-Portrait as Prey

Wet,
you wanted me to
fold in half, arms
behind my back
while I act
like I like you
liking that

Self-Portrait as South Carolina Morning

Look, a trash bag.
My friend
isn't my lover, nor
is my lover.
I'll lay on the ground
for the open air
and woodenness.
I plan to.
So to no longer care
can't happen.
I'll see.

Self-Portrait as Curtain Blowing into a Room

I fold a red dress
in a smaller world blocked
by cardboard boxes.
I set up for myself.
A man's back
to me, in bed.
It's after.
It's only night.
The place is a countdown.

Self-Portrait as Little Rote Exercise

I pick a fossil up and it is
replaced by a
fossil.
Not just ice:
I run over ice
I slip
I slip to run this past
past you.
Love you.

Self-Portrait as Canyon

Your black car
drove here.
I swore I wouldn't
know you and then
some, back roads.
An eagle. A baby. The Statue of Liberty.
A back room is sepia, not dirty.

Self-Portrait as Works and Days

Kissing you
was like tending a tiny
desktop garden
of fake succulents.
I took a photo.

Self-Portrait as Folding Chair

You flipped me upside
down at closing
time. I was important
to be identical.
And lingering, like a lobby, a delicate
rug in that.

Self-Portrait as Pictures on a Screen

Younger guy
in glossy loafers
I see you.
Stinks in here.
With a palm tree.
A washer machine.
Quickie on the lid
to redistribute
missingness?

Self-Portrait as Drinking Water Sampling Station

I won't forfeit
desire.
Whip in hand.
If my inner life
is so sustainable, might
I not mistake
public utility
with me
you
ordinary morning.
Now kneel.
Ledge
of the torso, you
can't say I.

Self-Portrait as Etymological Dictionary

A real body does
return.
That's him, lounging.
Meager beard.
I don't need to know the word for fraud
to look it up.
I look up.
The yellow light
throughout my apartment.
Or how do you
say jealousy.

Self-Portrait as Goldfish and Sculpture

You and me
we're on the red sofa.
The whole room
participates.
You won't. Why?
Small grass
gets dizzy.
Off-kilter tact.
Plump instantiation.
Here. Here.
In here.

Self-Portrait as Shovel

Take me back.
What'd dirty you
falls through my head.
You lifted me.
Bent over
to put me in and over
the earth. The
earth.
I don't own this yard.

Self-Portrait as C Change

An orange could be crushed.
I'd forgotten that.
What else?
Be average, pink stapler.
A window was difficult, I folded
underneath
underneath

Self-Portrait as Birdhouse

Everything constructed
is constructed
says me. I'm small.
You might as well be hopping off.
Flapping.
A plastic outline.
Now drop that water bottle cap.
That's separatism.

Meditation in an Emergency

Per my compassion concussion, I was getting hit by the sight of an old man stooped on a stoop in a purple pull-over and scraggly eyes, when a slumpy boy toddling in a two-tonnish feather coat and a pom-pom cap like a bell tower came by, and *he* was going past a blue recycling bin on its side from the wind, frozen water in waves on the street, one patch of ice looking like dried white semen, that's how white it looked, otherwise the ice looked like ice, pale and smokey.

Sonnet XXXIV

Even Shakespeare opens
up some question of his lover
cuz he can't get the bitter stuff
dislodged, either 'Why didst thou promise
such a beauteous day?' or betrayal's a hand to stick
in '[a]nd make me travel forth without my cloak.' Some like
to stick it in for that froth, but Shakespeare breaks. My heart's the most
when he is plain. Vis a vis protection from the elements, gear for the
outing, the sticky charge he lobs becomes ammo, so
I think his lover brave to 'let base clouds o'er
take [him] in [his] way / [h]iding thy bravery
in their rotten smoke.'

Good Night

I'd better go.
Killzone spraytanned,
I inked two cute Welsh guys with swords.
My good depth-breath
ticks on, stick-ish,
and guys flank me, whose person
cuts G O A L S.
                     Wishing
forward, two wicked types, ferried.
I'd go and tell super fast
and pee on, reckless schoolboy.
I uttered two wish-totals, one per guy.
Add ink; it opens from two knives.

Against Professional Secrets

We'd already been having a miserable time when my father ordered our ingrate of a brother to school. Cured of love, a little late in rainy February, my mother served some yams in the basement. We were seated at the table of my dad and my older brothers. And my mother sat herself down at our feet in the same gesture that a fireplace does, in a house. We touched the door.

> 'The door's been touched!'—my mother.
> 'The door's been touched!'—my own mother.
> 'The door's been touched!'—said all parts of my mother.

Walk on, native daughter, *a* daughter, to see who's shown up this time, said me (sounding yucky like Telemachus).

And, without waiting to see who'd shown up to take the maternal slot, A., my brother, the son who'd left to see the world but now left to see who'd shown up this time, opened the door.

The weather took over my family. Mom got cold and distant. She made it to the patio outside. She was the cold and the distance. If you're picturing clouds right now, you're halfway there.

Then pain and Pavlov's dogs touched their noses to the front door.

'Because I didn't tell you to leave! The door opens! Be native, daughter,' I heard A. tell one of the dogs. His own dog.

This is all to say this is how I came to throw up my middle finger to the distress of the subjunctive, distress of my father, revealing the man I am in pluperfect rain. He could at the drop of a hat turn on the waterworks so that the windows would seem late by the way they shine.

However:

'And tomorrow, in school,' dissertated Dad, magisterially before a public made of his weekend sons.

And so, the law, the cause of the law. And so it was all my life.

Mom could have maybe cried, with the shame of her own mother. None of us wanted to eat. Would you have been able to keep your appetite in such a circumstance? The lips of Dad seemed culpable for leaving something broken, a final purse that he knew about. In the mouths of brothers, an absorbed migraine of children. The margarine of summer had already melted.

I left that banal house of water, dizzy from the patio. Such a bad visit. A little too much for me this time. I felt neither too far away nor too thinkable, without being brutal. A clock felt like it was lodged in my throat. But really it was an old shawl, one from Mom's drawers, a pattern of chickens on it that hadn't incubated any eggs yet (I took the scarf to wrap around my head because I had a headache, heralding my skill of tying something tight across my temples.) I'd forgotten the incident instantly, the scarf was part of the life of her children. It was cold for the cows and all of the eggs. A clucking lasted after its verb.

No one spoke to me in Hebrew at home, only English. And about wanting to speak to me in more than one tongue, no one left me a sign that it was left in them, a hot-cold meal Mom made.

'Where are the kids of the old chicken?'
'Where are the chickens of the old chicken?'

Poor things. Where could they be.

Apology

I picked up my bluest pen, put a star
beside the best parts of a poem I loved.

Each little star made me make this my
self, then, out of looking out for cruelty.

Dear man, I tried singing, it doesn't speak
to yr tenderness to indicate yr heart

is being busy breaking from the sight
of someone combing through trash to

find food. Put it at the end of yr longing
you have the tiny balls to call a hymn.

I looked up to life. Long distance availability.
Stupidity of poetry. I had this need,

in the long run, to form a couplet with a
someone. I was getting on a train.

December. Cool pines, stubby grates. Cracks,
sighs, caresses, twigs, breaths of a squirrel.

Night offering the shadowy subway car glass, itself
an example. I was busy bringing my self

home to you, a central dumbness of poems
navigating systems and rules outside

themselves. Or: I was busy bringing my poem
home to you, a central dumbness of self

navigating systems, and rules outside themselves.
But even to sum up what we do seems too

unpoemed, I mean unpeopled, by the loneliest
light of the stars. It's by them I can't see.

How I Wrote Certain of My Books

Flipping the channel, I came to set my eyes on a tennis star lancing the green ball. I was feeling ashamed of the criticism I had made of well-meaning others who had moved around me, as if in a game involving a green ball. Click. I couldn't control it. The same click happens in the brain. In other other words, I know myself first and foremostly through my body exercising functions minus malice multi-taskishly. The hand. The heart that lets the hand make its first to final move. A flip to this from the hand that every translation is, in this case, Don Bartlett's, of Karl Ove Knausgaard: 'For the heart, life is simple; it beats for as long as it can. Then it stops.' I'm here to affirm that in the precise moment in which each organ functions, the human has the chance to be a big believer. Malice no longer seems like the only option. That is to say, I became a real translator. I said something different. Even now I'm shaking that.

FATHER FIGURES

Today I saw

Jon Hamm

shirtless

on a beach

reading Dante

translated by

John Ciardi

Versus the one

by Mandelbaum

I'm reading

Or that I once

believed

my mind was small

I saw a man

now and his

old blonde lab

I saw big air

turn inside out

I saw wind

blow notecards I'd

put words on Words

old as ever

put on paper

Jon Hamm shirtless

on a beach

reading Dante

John Ciardi

The wind blew the

many notecards

off my wooden

desk Blew toward

the opposite side

of the room I

turn out to be

    No I turn out

to be the space

I write in

The wind chose words

    I saw the perfect

body was

hairy Bulbous

where I'd handle

him On a gust

As for me I

once was a bird

Ever making

a homey spot

That here was where

I went for that

Dad neighbor type

in muscle shirt

His three kids

trampolined their

glee It's nothing

to do with me

Having that Dad

all to myself

Momentary

    Pink blossom tree

two yards over

rips Pulls in wind

'On Wanting To

Have a Child' I

might title my

spell

    The pink tree

confuses me

    Dad's left hand in

pocket The right

he lets the boy

pull on A

latest find 'in

the new world' to

riff off Jorie

Graham

    Her green

hardback selected

flutters open

by my hand

    I'm a new sound

A cardinal

zips its line through

my sight A line

as divides these

areas off

What is the point

of the oh so

pointed leaves I

heckle the out

-line of

The sun

crimps each

poinsettia

So that drifting

for a slowed-down

poem About

my yard Random

people A fear

I must be near

Now that's the point

       I come back

into the yard

via the white cat

a neighbor called

Sat like nope Got

on all fours in

response to her

voice Neighbor gave

up Closed that door

Cat rose and turned

around to go

around I laughed

Tight or other

-wise in prose Same

people rarely

learn

Neighbor o

-pens door Cat

streaks into house

A non-Dad joke

could go like

this A thing is

about its own

circumference

A pink gnarled blos

-som sum of seeds

is better to get

feeling into

words Words keep wind

You open your

mouth to say them

A photo can't

    Put your fingers

to each temple

and press and close

your eyes When my

Dad died my Mom

needed me to

do that Words

keep wind

Talking more trash

is not a bad

idea Let's

quote Homer in

The Odyssey

'Antinous

you are a lord

but what you say

is trash' Or that's

the translator

Emily Wil-

son's haul of it

I hauled trash out

today to curbs

'Today I made

more of it than

you I'm sure' said

my neighbor A.

to up the ante

of our I guess

discourse

It is like trash

to do pushups

for Instagram

School Dude Login's

the website Mom

points out

'The IT guys

are such sexists'

'Such trash'

That was the trash

near me today

    Mistaking my

worth with that gain

now neighbor boy

plays his dog He

scares me Running

to collapse be

-low the dog He

aims his pointed

finger at her

blam blam blam Ouch

This poem can't

predict outcome

    Leaping her mouth

should she fear him

Boy wears headphones

What has he been

listening to

    No buds are in

my ears I've been

inside my ear

my whole life

    I'm going to

shut out who else

to decide this

A yellow truck

turns past us all

two golden

retrievers

on a run with

some blonde I'll call

Doug

Infinitudes

of Dougs

before I'm game

to be his yet

Wet I'll get off

Who my last hook

up was I can't

remember but

I felt like the

false bottom

of a drawer

He was like

Tap tap What's here

No more sex for

you said the gods

Stiff daffodils

that I reach out

for before I

have a kind word

to say of them

I stuck my head

between his legs

I'm his one

orange hammock

Such as in my

neighbor's yard

I could have sworn

is new It isn't

    Once poets put

names on things Now

I take them off

    Words keep wind

I text these words

My hand's siding

with motion

What of the red

robe I see

Homer says

wife of Hector

wove at her loom

Andromache

You were there when

news of your

husband's death rose

in your walled town

'like inhuman fire'

One of Homer's

go-to phrases

Let's say phases

Now no doubt robes

of dark red fold

themselves

Homer re:

grief you told me

it's a desire

stirred within by

a god

And Thetis

stirred it among

soldiers deep for

Patroclus No

equivalent

You Homer

you put one foot

before the next

on glistening

sand

How far off

from where you grew

up Up and down

my homeyard I

put my gaze on

I so grew up

Wind in the grass

that yes is green

btw gleam

that twitches in

-sects

    Far be it from

me to not believe

it's zooming to

me now Some

-where somehow Grief

and a blade

you don't hand me

but because of

you I hear

      I hear

the poplar tree

someone fells in

The Iliad

It wags an

iron axe I

take to the house

I live in now

on Poplar Ave

    It's one foot

in front of the

other I am

    I close my eyes

Blind eye and

shimmer

    When I open

my eyes there's

some jogger

His blue suit brags

about getting

to hold him No

that jogger won't

turn me on He's

not memory

    To be out of

time's my new kink

    Mesmerized

by his pics that

make the cotton

blue shirt strain

I'm picky to

the melody

His lips

Even porn would

work more than this

poem to show

off a stranger

I predict this

one bird upon

my porch

Two have landed

on my swinging

love seat One

juttishly looks

at the other

with straw in beak

The jut of head

suggests a

mechanical

cop-out A

fluid head turn such

as I put off

my moneyed tasks

and jerk in new

positions I'm

no expert in

Came one came all

is what I'll say

to birds Not friends

I eyes closed head

turned under a

heavy today

    Two birds one swing

one me putting

it on Paper

blame game

Curl against wind

    The fantasy

was me and Cruz

Lito Cruz with

his perfect worn

father figure

vibe but I step

aside my will

I'm not green

The snow says

on the swing

I have a how

do you say it

tendency

A sky at my

mouth

Like a dog's bark

Pair of brackets

I now put what

some might say is

secondary

stuff into

just to spill

I have to

    I'm like snow

Sulked under

the sun it is

becumming

    But if this sex

implies trust

let's recall

what Homer says

One day

a cheater walks

in What lets her

smile after she's

caught in a bed

with what's his face

in golden chains

Homer says

she leaves

for her private

island where oil

organic stuff

cedar citrus spice

gets rubbed on her

by assistants

who are unpaid

interns at core

the Graces

The guy's ripped

No shame reddens

his cute visage

His ribbon core

You Homer say

he leaves for Thrace

His altar waits

The story ends

on her looking

gorgeous

in clothes I can't

afford

But I can tell

this story Say

something morbid

like all we do

Some dramas don't

depend on death

They depend on

sound

        Carly Rae

Jepsen uses

her tongue

to touch the tip

of her teeth when

she sings The sound

system of my

neighbor A.

cuts the spring air

Juicy chorus

some two doors down

I hear the cutting

through

    Neighbor cleans

His yard works him

out I'm here for

her pushy lips

Some video

I watched once where

Carly Rae and

cute abs guy flirt

in a garage

mine resembles

That Dad neighbor

mows his yard when

-ever he likes

Stops Yells

Pink plastic chair

he thudded on

with his mower

Constant presence

keeps real gladness

true to a life

I am in Like

when my friend M.

texts there's some

always life

we haven't

lived and won't and

beyond OK

    I don't know who

needs to hear this

but now Dad's stooped

again to pick

up a brown chair

his own size

    With one hand I'm

him A rare state

    I say OK

Kid turns herself

upside down

Good for her She

seems not to care

her belly shows

    She reminds me

of a pigtailed

Athena play

-ing a girl who

skips ahead of

Odysseus

to lead him part

of the way home

    Don't be a man

who only talks

to great dead men

is the message

I picked up from

a mirror book

by my mentor

    Don't only talk

to the dead Not

at the expense

of the people

living before

you Mary Jo

you're right I'm in

my bed with hard

-cover books

Dante Larry

Kramer Homer

Susan Sontag

Zadie Smith John

Ashbery Anne

Carson Amy

Tan Claudia

Rankine Herman

Melville Mayer

Bernadette but

three cute otters

M. texts are cute

three and all there

unbuttoning

Life online is

of stronger stuff

I gaze at green

gaps My garden's

gaps amaze me

Sticking my face

Shiny spots when

a gust guzzles

Words keep Wind

sponsors my cross

-talk So I cross

my one backyard

to tomorrow

I put my red

fake slip-ons on

Red as blood

pretends to be

when not inside

itself I got

these shoes as a

gift from a man

who once broke

my front door

He shouldered it

to get out Door

only opened

inward Damage

did yes include

a case of

gonorrhea

    Red slip-ons won't

always come through

Like Dante's do

when he goes on

a guided tour

to find his love

The underworld

of pollsters

Politicians

Shades of ex-loves

    What does Dante

do He sticks out

His feet make dust

move Make sound

Nor am I dead

That's why I'm loud

about my sex

    Dante also is

himself on a

beast's back

Which I love

It wheels him

and his teacher

who also read

Homer hard

through a dark

then drops them down

resignedly

The beast kicks up

back into air

quick as an eel

through a dark pond

or an arrow

from a wide bow

    Although I know

how to shoot I

rarely do Who

should I shoot at

My enemies

I spare them

I leave them be

    Someone taught me

as a desert

does the sand to

be extra dry

    Someone texts me

Which is more

painful to lose

A pet or child

    One day we all

we will all know

somehow at once

comparison's

no true friend

Swift and direct

hitting a nail

on someone's head

Most days fall

headfirst like fish

into a real lake

I sun myself

beside A thread

to pick upon

A dust fleck

in only wind

But let's compare

this work of

staying afloat

to Ulysses

telling Dante

it mattered more

to travel than

stay at home

with wife son dad

    Longing isn't

discovery

'[T]he vice and worth

of men' happens

on Poplar Ave

    I was there

I saw a man

and his old lab

Gray thin hair

Was tan Big pecs

Why couldn't he

have been the one

who told Dante

this old story

I say he could

He could

Perfect dark zone

The sequence I

Plus chimes

My neighbor's hung

Finally I did

suck him off Who's

to say I did

not

    The branch

I am was dropped

from a tree but

branch hits house

House isn't made

of wood

    Someone

told me poems

change the person

writing them and

no one else This

is how

I'll drink my head

No longer call

leading this life

'approaching

the narrows'

as Ulysses

does the landscape

he and his men

headed to when

what circled them

four times and then

yanked them down

was a blue wave

lips go dumb from

Notes

'My Poems Won't Change the World' is inspired by Patrizia Cavalli's poem of the same name, translated by Jorie Graham.

'The Wanderer's Nightsong' is inspired by a poem of the same name by Johann Goethe.

'Invisible Cities' is inspired by a poem of the same name by Arthur Rimbaud.

The 'Self-Portraits' series is inspired by work by Robert Rauschenberg, Edward Hopper, Henri Matisse, George Sugarman, Nancy Spero, César Vallejo, Hesiod, Gabriel Orozco, the City of New York Department of Sanitation, and David Hockney.

'Joy, Memory, Novitiate of Passion' is inspired by Hilda Hist's poem of the same name, translated by Beatriz Bastos.

'Good Night' is inspired by a poem of the same name by William Carlos Williams.

'Meditation in an Emergency' is inspired by the poem of the same name by Frank O'Hara.

'Against Professional Secrets' is inspired by a poem of the same name by César Vallejo, translated by Joseph Mulligan.

'Apology' is inspired by 'Merry Christmas from Hegel' by Anne Carson.

'How I Wrote Certain of My Books' takes its title from an essay of the same name by Raymond Roussel.

Acknowledgements

Thanks to the editors the following journals for publishing earlier versions of some of these poems:

American Chordata
"Self-Portrait as Curtain Blowing into a Room"

Art and Understanding
"Self-Portrait as Pictures on a Screen"
"Self-Portrait as South Carolina Morning"
"Self-Portrait as Canyon"

Changes Review
"The Wanderer's Nightsong"
"Sonnet XXXIV"
"Good Night"
"[When I open]" from "Father Figures"

Denver Quarterly
"Apology"
"[Today I saw]" from "Father Figures"

Figure1
"Self-Portrait as Drinking Water Sampling Station"

Posit
"Self-Portrait as Works and Days"
"Self-Portrait as Prey"
"Self-Portrait as Shovel"
"Self-Portrait as Little Rote Exercise"

Tyger Quarterly
"Joy, Memory, Novitiate of Passion"
"Invisible Cities"

The Lincoln Review
"[A non-Dad joke]" from "Father Figures"

LAY OUT YOUR UNREST